THE LITTLE BOOK OF
CHAOS

Craig Brown

D0449915

WARNER BOOKS

For Frances

A *Warner* Book

First published in Great Britain by Warner Books 1998
Reprinted in 1998 (five times)

A CIP catalogue record for this book is
available from the British Library.

ISBN 0 7515 2657 6

Typeset in Stone by M Rules
Printed and bound in Great Britain by William Clowes Ltd

Warner Books
A Division of
Little, Brown and Company (UK)
Brettenham House
Lancaster Place
London WC2E 7EN

*I've penned this little book to be a
source of much irritation to you
and your friends.
Keep it in your pocket at all times
and refer to it when calm threatens.*

*Those who follow its advice
will find themselves
on edge.*

*And if they cannot irritate themselves
then at least they can irritate others.*

*Open this book
and step into a world
of petty grievance.*

REGAIN THE CHILD WITHIN

The adult world is filled with tension.
Regain the child within.
Pull a colleague's hair
and when she yells
'ARGH! He HURT me!'
remember to yell back,
'But she STARTED it!'

WHITE

The clothes you wear
influence
your recollection of each passing day.

So wear white whenever you cook
and you will remember every ingredient
until the sun goes down.

LIGHT A CANDLE IN YOUR BATH

Before climbing into your bath,
surround it
with bright flaming candles.
Some may set fire to the curtains;
others may scald your behind;
still others may fizzle out after a splash,
causing you much
vexation.

WELCOME A GOLDFISH

We can learn much
from the kingdom of the fish.
A goldfish brought home in a plastic bag
can teach us powers of observation
as it circles around aimlessly
before dying three months later
after you have left it behind
for a long weekend.

TAKE TIME WHEN
READING A MAP

When your partner is driving along a
motorway,
wait
until the car has just passed
the correct exit
before stating firmly,
'That was the right one'.

CHAFE YOUR PRIVATE PARTS

In Chafe Therapy, garments of
100% nylon
are recommended for a complete chafing
of all your private parts.

INCREASE YOUR AWARENESS

Be aware of what is
going on at all times.
Before retiring to bed, tune into
CNN News for the latest update
of horrors around the world.

HARKEN TO THE TUNE WITHIN

When all is silent around you, strive
to remember a tune that reached
number 17 in the charts in 1973.
Whistle half the chorus,
over and over again,
all day long.

As the sun goes down,
those of your friends and colleagues
who did not know the tune
will now know it
by heart.

Pamper Your Feet

Spread jojoba oils on your feet.
Massage your feet with creams from
seven continents.
Pummel them with luxurious lotions.
Now put on your socks.

They will adhere to you wheresoever you
journey.

THE REWARD

Dieting?
Reward yourself at frequent intervals
with half-pound bars
of dairy milk chocolate.

YOUR DOG LOVES PEOPLE

Your dog loves people.
Let him demonstrate his affection
for your friends
by encouraging him to roger
their knees.

LIFE, TOO, IS CIRCULAR

Life is circular.
And so too is a roll of sellotape.
Always let the sellotape stick
back on itself
between applications.

For by so doing, you will enjoy
the search for the lost end
and you will appreciate
that life, too, is circular.

WHEN TWO OR MORE ARE GATHERED

When two or more are gathered
around the TV set,
be sure to gain hold of the
remote-control
and click it every three to four seconds.

ONE NOTCH

Maintain your belt,
brassiere and buckled shoes
one notch too tight
to secure your discomfort
for the day ahead.

LEARN TO BREATHE

In the midst of office mayhem,
enrich your life by taking deep, deep
breaths.
Your colleagues will also benefit
from the sound
of your relaxation.

PIT YOUR WITS

Pit your wits against the vicissitudes
and vagaries of fortune by
remembering to set off between ten and
fifteen minutes late for those
urgent appointments.

FOR THE SAKE OF YOUR
FELLOW PASSENGERS

When journeying on a train
keep in touch
by dialling your office
on your mobile phone
and bellowing,
loud and clear,
for the sake of your fellow passengers,
'Hi! I'm on a train!'

REMAINING ALERT

How to remain alert, even when
sipping a soothing mug of tea?
Find a broken mug.
Glue its handle back on.

Now, whenever you
sip tea from this cup
you will feel on red alert.

Presents for the Kiddies

There is nothing like
an electric stylophone,
a drum kit, or a music centre with a
choice of
twenty-five different disco beats
to make your friends remember
exactly who it was who gave
their children
those presents.

A WELCOMING PLACE

Your fridge is a
welcoming place.
Fill it with many separate saucers
half-balanced on one another containing
four pieces of ravioli,
two spoonfuls of rice pudding,
a cracked egg and
eleven baked beans.

SLEEP LIKE A BABY

Sleep like a baby:
wake up every two to three hours
soaking wet
and bawling for food.

DAMP

Maintain a roll of damp toilet paper
for your visitors,
leaving them to ponder whether
it fell into
the toilet.

LEARNING TO CARE

If you are a doctor
or a health visitor,
always remember
to call breasts
boobs.

FOUR SEASONS

While callers wait to be put through,
let them listen to
Vivaldi's *Four Seasons*.

COVER YOUR WOUND

Whenever you sustain an injury
take care
to use the type of Elastoplast
that rips hairs from your skin
when you remove it
and leaves a dirty glue-like residue
for weeks after.

SOMEONE WE CAN LEAN ON

We all need someone we
can lean on.

So make sure you lean on
your partner
when walking up
a steep hill.

BE SURE

Distribute matchboxes
around your home.

But first be sure that they are filled
with spent matches.

LOYAL FRIENDS

Your friends have remained close by you
while you smoked cigarettes, pipes
and cigars,
while you broke wind and burped
and while you sang
'Bohemian Rhapsody'.
But all is not lost.
Have you tried snuff?

CATCH YOURSELF

Catch yourself
unexpectedly
on a doorknob,
by wearing a dressing gown
with large bell sleeves.

BEFORE LEAVING YOUR PLACE OF WORK

Before leaving your place of work for
the weekend
be sure to set the burglar alarm
to ring
until your return.

SOAKING

When seeking to soothe away
the cares of the day,
climb into your bath
when it is still lukewarm,
immediately before
the hot water runs out.

Now remain where you are –
too chilly to get out
too chilly to stay in.

SHOW YOUR SATISFACTION

After supping ale,
always show your satisfaction
by going,
'Warrrgghhhhhh!'
and wiping your mouth with your sleeve.

MUCH TO LEARN

We have much to learn from other
animals.
In the height of summer, visit the
Highlands and Islands.
And learn much from
the little mosquito.

A NECESSARY ADDENDUM

Upon leaving the cinema,
while others are swapping
their favourite scenes,
remember to say,
'It wasn't nearly as good as the book'.

AUTUMNAL HUES

Add an autumnal hue
to your armchair or sofa
by storing an apple-core
down the side
and leaving it to
mature.

AFTER EACH DEEP SLEEP

After each deep sleep,
make a careful note of your
dreams
and recite them, in great detail,
to those you encounter,
always beginning,
'There was this, well, this
sort of *thing* . . .'

WHEN APPROACHED BY A WEARY TRAVELLER

When approached by a weary traveller
for directions,
take care to describe his route in the
greatest
possible
detail
before adding,
'Actually, I've just thought of
a better way'.

GO PLACIDLY

Go placidly into each noisy party,
always using your softest voice.
This way, those to whom you speak
will only catch
every third word,
and they will feel obliged to interject,
'Really?',
to show that they understand
what on earth
you are on about.

To welcome a friend

Before that special friend enters
your home,
prepare your children to give him or her
that extra-special welcome
by placing a Gameboy in their hands.

THE WORLD IS AT PEACE

A sunny day.
Happiness reigns.
The birds chirrup in the trees.
Family and friends chat warmly.
The world is at peace with itself.
Why not ruin it all with a barbecue?

An immutable sign

Life leaves its own rich patina
upon your clothes.
Preserve these memories by taking your
clothes to a dry cleaners.
They will be returned looking exactly the
same, but now
covered in safety pins, and in labels
saying,
WE HAVE BEEN
UNABLE TO REMOVE THESE STAINS
COMPLETELY.

WATCH THE GRASS GROW

Purchase a lawn-mower with a pull-start.
Pull. And pull. And pull. And pull. And
pull.
And pull. And pull. And pull. And pull.
Now collapse.
And watch the grass grow.

An oasis

Your videotape recorder provides
an oasis of chaos
in a world riddled with calm.
Be sure to let its digital numbers flash

⑆**00·00**⑆
⑆**00·00**⑆
⑆**00·00**⑆

over and over and over again
throughout the day,
all day, everyday.

GOING ANYWHERE NICE THIS SUMMER?

Pay a visit to your hairdresser
or to your dentist.
Sit back.

And wait for this question to be asked.

WHEN DRIVING THROUGH A QUIET VILLAGE

When driving through a quiet village,
turn the volume of your new
heavy metal CD
to its very highest:
CHUGGACHUGGACHUGGACHUGGA.
Then sit back, with a worldly expression
on your face
and slap your steering wheel knowingly
in time with the beat.

WISDOM

There is much wisdom
to be garnered from
those who have lived many years
upon this extraordinary planet of ours.
So heed ye well the advice of
Michael Winner.

DA-DA-DUM **DUM DUM**

Upon spying
a piano in a
friend's house,
be sure to play
the opening bars of 'Chopsticks',
over and over and over
and over and over
again.

THE JOURNEY OF LIFE

Leave no more than two minutes
to buy your ticket before catching a train.
And be sure to queue behind the man
who wishes to find out
the exact route, times and price of
a ticket from Aberystwyth to Fort
Augustus, taking in Bodmin, Swindon,
Basingstoke
and York,
using a Senior Citizen's Family Railcard
that's two-and-a-half weeks out of date.

JINGLE, JANGLE

Chatting informally?
Let the world resound to the
jangling of loose change
in your trouser pockets.

TUCKING UP

A chilly night.
A warm bed.
You have finished a good book.
You sigh contentedly.
You switch off the light.
Peace. Perfect peace.

But did you remember to turn off the
oven?

GOOD OF YOU

The photos come back
from the chemist.
Your friend stares at one in blank horror.
She looks
cross-eyed, red-faced, 30 stone and
close to death.
Reassure her by saying,
'That's good of you!'

A CAMPFIRE

No need for matches!
Just rub two sticks together for
half an hour
and
Hey Presto!
You will feel very hot.

A FRIENDLY NOTE

Employers!
Employ many people called John
in your place of work,
so that when you call one
the others all look up.

A TICKLE IN YOUR THROAT

A tickle in your throat?
Book the very best seat in the theatre
and enjoy a good cough.

ADD INTEREST TO YOUR PERSONALITY

Do people ignore you?
Why not cultivate a handlebar
moustache?

It could provide an invaluable
talking-point.

THINK OF OTHERS

Always maintain a steady
70mph
in the fast lane
so that your fellow drivers
are not tempted to break the speed limit.

A BESEECHING EYE

Never let a friend sit down
to eat
without placing a dog
at the corner of the table
to observe his every
mouthful
with a beseeching eye.

EVEN IN YOUR DARKEST HOURS

Though most commonly associated
with the 1970s,
Dr Scholl sandals are still widely available
in chemist shops throughout the land.
Purchase a pair.
Their clackety noise will be your
companion,
even in your darkest hours.

THE INNER PERSON

A shiny metal ring strategically placed
through the bottom lip,
the tongue, the eyebrow or
the cheek,
will help bring out
the inner person.

KEEP IN TOUCH

Keep in touch with friends and
acquaintances
by posting them all a chain letter
beginning,
'Welcome to a marvellous opportunity!
Pedro aged 33 from Brazil
ignored this letter.
Just 22 days later, he died.'

THE IMAGINATION IS A WONDERFUL THING

Before embarking on
a long journey,
take steps to tear the relevant
map
from your road atlas.

The imagination is a wonderful thing.

A WELCOME INTERRUPTION

It is 6.45pm.
All over the nation,
your fellow citizens are relaxing after
another hard day's work.
Some are chatting, others eating
or drinking
or watching TV.
Now is the time to phone
and inform them they have been selected
for a once-in-a-lifetime special offer
on prestige double-glazing.

FOREVER FRESH

Before departing a friend's home,
remember to leave behind
your child's favourite teddy-bear,
an urgent letter in an unstamped
envelope,
a purse and a pair of wellington boots.
As they gather them up,
wrap them, seal them,
stamp them and post them,
the image of your face will remain
forever in their minds.

THE WAY TO HIS HEART

Paris in the Spring.
You visit a bar, bustling with ordinary
French people, all ready with their orders.
Do not worry that you do not
know the language:
simply speak loudly to Le Patron
in pidgin English,
putting on a funny French accent
and gesticulating wildly.

A NEW UMBRELLA

Carry an umbrella with you
wheresoever you venture,
leave it behind, then
forget where you left it,
thus ensuring the need
to buy a new one.

THE JOURNEY

It is the journey, not the getting there,
that is important.
To halt regularly along life's pathway,
first check your shoes are threaded
with circular nylon shoelaces.

Two Thoughtful Presents

Stuck for gift ideas for
two children of a friend?
Give one of them
a pet cat,
and the other
a pet mouse.

GREETING

Upon greeting a dear old friend
who's been through the wars,
look sympathetic and say,
'How are your spirits?
Low?'

THE GREEN BADGE OF COURAGE

Out on a first date?
Being interviewed for that important
new job?
A few skeins of spinach
stuck to the front teeth
will provide a reassuring badge
of identity.

THE TRUTH IS I NEVER LEFT YOU

Store managers!
Speed up your customers
by playing a light orchestral version of
'Don't Cry For Me Argentina'
over your crackly intercom.

LIVEN THINGS UP

If your dinner party is growing sticky,
liven things up by reciting
the Monty Python Dead Parrot sketch
in a variety of amusing voices.

KEEP A SECRET

Say to a friend,
'I've got such an amazing secret
to tell you
but
I'd better not because I
promised I wouldn't'.

PETROL PUMP

When filling your car with petrol
try to select a pump which
every few seconds
will click and stop pumping.

MAKE NEW FRIENDS

On moving to a
village or small country town,
make yourself known
to the close-knit community
by bagging the front pew and
making sure you are
first up to communion.

Teenager?

You are aged?
Eighteen or under?
Be sure?
To add?
The interrogative?
To every?
Few words?

PHHPHHHWRAUUGHSNIFF-SNIFFSNIFFPHWRAUGH

Friends and strangers alike
rejoice in the sound of
a nose well-blown.

ON A LONG JOURNEY

On a long journey with children,
say 'McDonalds' within five minutes of
your departure.
Your children will enjoy lobbying you for
a Big Mac and french fries
for the next three and a half hours.

A NOVEL GIFT

Cheer up friends who have had
their house repossessed
by giving them a soothing present.
How about a
homing pigeon?

A SHARED ACTIVITY

When making love,
be sure to let your partner know
the joy you share.
Every now and then
laugh out loud.

SHARING

There is nothing so conducive to
friendship
as eating out and
splitting the cost.

Cement the friendship
by gazing at the bill,
getting out your calculator
and saying,
'But I didn't have any mineral water'.

DEVOTION

Parking your car by a meter?
Feed the smallest amount into it,
thus ensuring you must return
at 12-minute intervals.

A BORN RACONTEUR

Do you have a favourite
humorous anecdote
you like to repeat
towards the end of dinner parties?
Repeat it once every two months for the
next thirty years, and on 180 separate
occasions your partner will be reminded
that they are living with
a born raconteur.

An Island of Calm

If a friend is
going mad
trying to find something,
be sure to remain an Island of Calm:
sit back in your chair,
sip gently at a cup of tea,
smile warmly and say,
'Now where did you last see it?'

THE KISS

Love does not arise without a struggle.
Kiss.
You suck; your partner sucks;
you both suck.
The dual-cyclone vacuum effect
stops you from breathing.

Only by suffering can we demonstrate
our love.

VISITING A FRIEND'S HOUSE

Everyone admires strength of character.
Whenever you visit a friend's house
for a meal
say, 'Just a little for me – I'm on a diet',
as the dish emerges from the oven.

BULLETIN

When asked,
'How are you?'
reply in full.

A WELCOME RESPONSE

When friends' children
refuse to eat what's on their plates,
lighten the atmosphere by exclaiming,
'I'm lucky! Mine eat everything!'

THE SECRET OF ETERNAL YOUTH

In the gap between two words
always insert
'Right?'

You have now gained the secret
of eternal youth.

THE PERFECT GUEST

When staying with a friend,
open and shut all the cupboards in
the kitchen.
When they say,
'What are you looking for?',
reply,
'Oh, don't worry, I'll soon find it'.

CHEERING UP A FRIEND

Is your friend feeling a bit low?
Give her that
I've-just-won-the-Grand-Prix
sensation
by shaking a can of Coke
very hard before
handing it to her.

A FINAL WORD

Always read loosely bound
paperbacks,
so that when you are reaching their
climax
and you turn over
the last-but-one
page
you find
the
last
sentence
doesn't

ABOUT THE AUTHOR

Craig Brown first came to prominence as the voice on the other end of the telephone that says 'Thank you for calling. You are being held in a queue'. His books include *The Magic of Weetabix: The Craig Brown Book of Country Cookery* and *If You'll Just Let Me Finish: A Biography of Michael Howard*. He is careful never to drive anywhere without leaving his right indicator flashing.

Email him on: .dot.craigbro.@.stresscenter.*.UK.scratchcard.@ stickysurfaces.esther.dot.exercisebike.@.dot.dot.dot.andonemoredot.